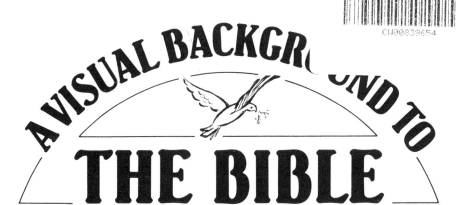

A VISUAL BACKGROUND TO THE BIBLE

A.G. PATSTON

Illustrated by the author

RELIGIOUS EDUCATION PRESS

A Division of Pergamon Press

The Religious Education Press
A Division of Pergamon Press
Hennock Road, Exeter EX2 8RP

Pergamon Press Ltd
Headington Hill Hall, Oxford OX3 0BW

Pergamon Press Inc.
Maxwell House, Fairview Park, Elmsford, New York 10523

Pergamon Press Canada Ltd
Suite 104, 150 Consumers Road, Willowdale, Ontario M2J 1P9

Pergamon Press (Australia) Pty Ltd
P.O. Box 544, Potts Point, N.S.W. 2011

Pergamon Press GmbH
Hammerweg 6, D-6242 Kronberg,
Federal Republic of Germany

First published 1981

Printed in Great Britain by A. Wheaton & Co. Ltd, Exeter
ISBN 0 08-025625-2 non net
ISBN 0 08-025626-0 net

Preface

This book is designed to give readers an insight into what day-to-day life was like in biblical times. It follows the author's highly succesful series, *A Visual Bible* and *A Visual Story of Christianity*.

The book provides a background to the Old Testament and New Testament times, and links the everyday activities of the people to the words of the Bible and the teachings of Jesus. The contents are grouped into eleven sections, dealing with such subjects as clothes, the home, daily work, transport, people and measurement. Relevant Bible readings are provided, and each page contains a programme of further work. In addition, there is a map of Palestine, a list of important places and a follow-up quiz.

A controlled vocabulary is used throughout the book, the text being written for the lower ages in secondary schools and upper age ranges in primary schools.

A Visual Bible

A VISUAL OLD TESTAMENT Book One: From Abraham to Daniel
Includes twenty-one pictorial summaries of Old Testament characters such as Abraham, Jacob, Joseph, Moses, Joshua, Gideon and Elijah.

A VISUAL OLD TESTAMENT Book Two: Abraham to Division of the Kingdom
Covers the beginnings of Hebrew history going back to the time of myth and legend and moving into the early history of the Kingdom of Israel up to the death of Solomon.

A VISUAL OLD TESTAMENT Book Three: From the Division of the Kingdom
Covers the story of the history of the Hebrew nation from the time of Solomon through the period of the prophets and up to the end of the Old Testament.

A VISUAL NEW TESTAMENT Book One: Jesus, Mighty in Word and Deed
Twenty-one stories and twenty-one diagrams of the life of our Lord, covering his birth, early ministry, his teaching, his miracles, and his mighty acts and deeds.

A VISUAL NEW TESTAMENT Book Two: Saviour of the World
Continues the story of the life and teaching of Jesus from his tragic journey to Jerusalem and his crucifixion on Calvary, to his resurrection and triumphal ascension.

A Visual Story of Christianity

A VISUAL NEW TESTAMENT Book Three: All That Jesus Began
Covers the founding of the Christian Church by the Apostles under the power of the Holy Spirit, including the work of Peter, Philip and others.

A VISUAL STORY OF CHRISTIANITY Book One: The Church Spreads across Europe
In the same style as his *Visual Bible* series, the author traces the story of the Church from Pentecost to the Holy Roman Empire in twenty-one selected episodes, with diagrammatic pictures.

A VISUAL STORY OF CHRISTIANITY Book Two: Through Division towards Unity
Takes the story of Christianity from the Holy Roman Empire through the chequered career of divided Christendom to the ecumenical spirit of our own times.

Contents

THE CLOTHES THEY WORE

Men's clothes

In biblical times the men wore a long, loose-sleeved tunic with a belt of leather or cloth round the waist. The belt could be used to keep a knife or dagger in place. Over this was a long, straight robe with wide sleeves, perhaps fringed or woven in coloured stripes.

In winter, the garments were woollen and a cloak of camel or goatskin was worn against the cold winds; in summer the garments were of linen. A head-cloth bound with cord or a rope of wool protected the head.

At first, sandals were only soles tied to the feet with strings or thongs but, later, the feet were completely covered.

When working in the fields, the men 'girded' themselves by tucking up the tunic into the belt to leave their legs free for work.

The one thing that every Jew was supposed to wear, at times of prayer, was a shawl called a 'tallith', with a tassel at each corner which stood for the four consonants of God's name in Hebrew–Yahweh.

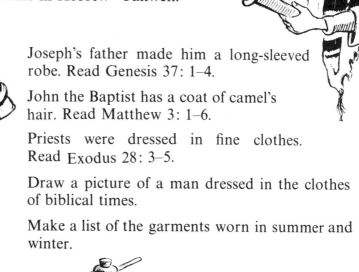

Joseph's father made him a long-sleeved robe. Read Genesis 37: 1–4.

John the Baptist has a coat of camel's hair. Read Matthew 3: 1–6.

Priests were dressed in fine clothes. Read Exodus 28: 3–5.

Draw a picture of a man dressed in the clothes of biblical times.

Make a list of the garments worn in summer and winter.

Women's clothes

The dress of women was almost the same as men, except for a veil. This sometimes almost completely covered the face, and an Eastern bride would always wear it so. The veil was worn over a close cap, often decorated with valuable coins. Cloth would be of finer material than that worn by men, and over a dress of soft silk a loose tunic was held in place by a gaily striped sash.

When Rebecca came out of the city at sundown to fill her pitcher at the well, she would have been dressed in a long simple robe, sashed at the waist, with a veil falling to the waist or draped around the neck. Perhaps she would have had ankle bracelets and a jewelled nose-ring.

Jewish women were expert in weaving wool and flax and dyeing the material in brilliant colours – scarlet, purple and blue. Purple was the most expensive and only rich families could afford purple garments. The colour came from a shellfish caught in the sea.

Clothes were washed by the side of a pool or river by kneading them against a stone.

A woman once lost one of her silver coins. Read Luke 15: 8–10.

Paul met a woman named Lydia, who was a dealer in purple fabric. Read Acts 16: 14–15.

Draw a picture of a woman dressed in the clothes of biblical times.

'A capable wife'. Read Proverbs 31: 10–25.

Describe, in your own words, the dress of women in biblical times.

Characters of the Bible

The Pharisees were people among the Jews who were very strict in keeping every custom and law. They were also very proud, and many were enemies of Jesus.

The Pharisees wore long fringes on their clothes and tassels on their shawls. The words of the Law were placed in little leather boxes which were strapped to the left arm and forehead.

The High Priest was the head or chief priest of the Jewish people. He wore a robe of blue over a white tunic. From his shoulders hung a gold breastplate, set with twelve jewels, on each of which was the name of one of the twelve tribes of Israel. On his head was a kind of mitre.

Samuel, when he was a boy, served in the Temple and helped a High Priest named Eli.

The Sadducees were richer and of higher rank than the Pharisees and were afraid that the people would try to make Jesus a king. Although they were usually enemies of the Pharisees, they joined with them to cause the death of Jesus.

God speaks to Samuel.
Read 1 Samuel 3: 1–18.

The parable of the Pharisee and the tax-gatherer. Read Luke 18: 9–14.

Jesus warns his disciples about the Pharisees and Sadducees. Read Matthew 16: 1–12.

Draw and colour a picture of a High Priest.

Answer these questions:
    What did the Pharisees wear?
    Why were the Sadducees afraid?
    Why did the Pharisees and Sadducees join together?

9

Tinkling ornaments

The people of Israel were fond of ornaments and jewellery. The head-dress of a rich woman could have gold chains fastened at the forehead and looped under the chin. The bracelets round her ankles might be joined with a chain so that she walked with little jingling steps.

Bracelets were also worn on the arms and they were usually flat bands or heavy twists of bronze or silver. There were rings for fingers and ears—and even toes—and there were many beautiful stones to choose from: pearls, emeralds, sapphires and rubies. Earrings were large, shaped in hoops and crescents.

Necklaces could range from shells or beads of stone to rich gold or bronze. A necklace was also a mark of honour; the King of Babylon gave Daniel 'a robe of purple and a chain of gold round his neck' (Daniel 5: 29).

Mirrors of polished metal were used and combs made of wood or ivory. There were even head-rests so that a woman could lie down without spoiling her 'hair-do'.

A merchant sold everything he had to buy a fine pearl. Read Matthew 13: 45–46.

Gold ornaments were taken from the enemy. Read Numbers 31: 48–50.

Read about the father who gave a ring to his son. Luke 15: 11–32.

Write the names of as many precious stones as you can remember.

Design a piece of jewellery to hang from a necklace.

HOMES

The houses they lived in

A house in Palestine was built of stone blocks covered with mortar or lime-mud. Sometimes, it was built round a courtyard paved with stone. In the centre was a well for water and, perhaps, a fig-tree growing against the wall.

An outside staircase led up to the flat roof and under the steps was often a stable for animals. The roof was made of branches and broad leaves covered with earth and usually it was not very strong. But in the better houses you could walk on the flat roof and there could be an 'upper room' for guests. There was a low wall round the roof for safety.

The houses were built so close together that the sunlight did not fall on the ground between them.

Only when he was sure of a visitor would a man open his front door. When he heard knocking, he went up to the roof and leaning over called 'Who?' A relative would answer 'Open', but a friend would say 'I'. If the voice was recognized the door was opened and the visitor made welcome.

Jesus used an upper room for the Passover Supper. Read Mark 14: 12–16.

'A house built on rock'. Read Matthew 7: 24–27.

Four friends of a paralysed man broke through a roof to get to Jesus. Read Mark 2: 1–5.

Make a model of a house in Palestine.

Write in your own words about the house built on rock and the house built on sand.

11

The family in the home

Inside the house there would be a single room with a raised part at one end on which the family slept.

It was dark and cool there with oil lamps standing in alcoves specially made for them. Usually the lamps were made of clay and the flame was never allowed to go out. The housewife who let her lamp oil burn away was thought to be careless or lazy.

During the winter the room was warmed by burning charcoal or wood in braziers made of iron.

Grandmother would sit in the raised part of the room to spin wool from goat's or camel's hair to make into fine cloth.

The furniture was very simple, consisting perhaps of a wooden chest for money or valuables and a low table and stools made of olive-wood. Cushions and rugs were used on the stone floor.

Martha and Mary welcomed Jesus to their home. Read Luke 10: 38–42.

Write the words of Psalm 119, verse 105: 'Thy word is a lamp to guide my feet and a light on my path.'

Draw a picture of an Eastern family inside their home.

'When a lamp is lit'. Read Matthew 5: 15–16.

Imagine you are a child living in these times and describe your home.

12

Food and cooking

A most important part of a home in biblical times was the kitchen. To bake fresh bread every day the corn had to be ground into flour in the corn-mill. The mill had two stones placed one on top of the other. One stone remained still while the upper stone was turned by a handle. Corn was put into a hole in the upper stone and ground between the two surfaces.

A loaf was a round, crisp cake of dough baked in an oven. This was little more than a hole in the wall in which a fire could be lit. Another way of baking bread was to heat an earthenware jar and then to put the thin loaves on the inside.

Goat's milk was churned into butter by shaking it up in a large leather bag.

Meat would be eaten only on feast days or festivals. It was made into a meat stew and served in a large bowl. Everyone helped themselves, eating with their fingers and mopping up the gravy with bread.

'Two women grinding at the mill'. Read Matthew 24: 39–44.

'My friend, lend me three loaves'. Read Luke 11: 5–10.

Write a few sentences to describe the making of bread.

'When you are having a party'. Read Luke 14: 12–14.

Draw a picture of two women grinding at the mill.

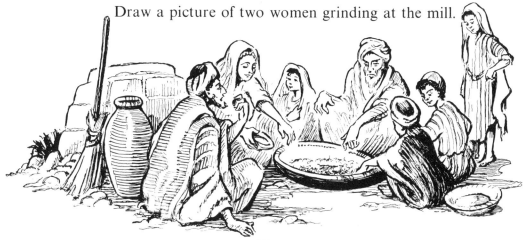

13

The water of life

In Canaan rain fell only twice a year, in October and March, and it quickly sank into the ground leaving the surface hard and dry.

Men had to learn how to dig to find water and make wells. A dug-out well was lined with stones and covered over with a rock to protect the water against the hot sun.

Every drop of rain-water was collected and stored in tanks called 'cisterns'. The Pool of Siloam in Jerusalem was one of these. Villages were built round a good water supply or spring and fetching water was the work of women.

To irrigate their fields the people raised water by wheels or a 'shadoof'. This was a weighted pole with a bucket at one end. The bucket was dipped into the river, the pole swung round and the water tipped out over the land.

In most of the towns and villages a water-seller sold water from a goatskin bag carried on his shoulder.

Eliezer found a wife for Isaac at a well. Read his prayer, Genesis 24: 11–14.

Read how Joseph was dropped into a dried-up well by his brothers. Genesis 37: 18–24.

Jesus told a blind man to wash in the Pool of Siloam and he was cured. John 9: 1–7.

Complete these sentences:
    In Canaan, rain fell . . . . . . a year.
    It rains in the months of . . . . . . and . . . . . .
    Rain-water was stored in tanks called . . . . . .

Draw a picture of a 'shadoof' and explain how it works.

14

The desert their home

The desert is a wilderness where nothing will grow and only in a few places is there water and grazing for animals. These places are called 'oases'.

Nomads are wandering people, moving with their flocks and herds in search of water. The Israelites were not true nomads, but they spent forty years wandering in the desert before they came to Canaan, the promised land. They lived in tents woven from black goat's hair, fastened by ropes and pegs (Isaiah 54: 2). The biggest tent was for the chief, and the first church, or tabernacle, of the Israelites was shaped like a tent.

When they moved from one place to another, the Israelites piled all their belongings on to the backs of donkeys. The camel was not used until later.

Often there were quarrels at the desert wells between the groups of shepherds, and desert tribes raided the Israelites for many years.

Desert shepherds quarrel over the wells. Read Exodus 2: 16–22.

Draw a picture of a tent in the wilderness.

How the desert tribes attacked the Israelites. Read Judges 7: 12–14.

'The Tent of the Presence'. Read Exodus 33: 7–11.

In your own words, describe what happened when Moses went to the Tent of the Presence.

THE DAILY WORK

Ploughing and sowing

Many people worked on the land and the life was very hard. The plough used by the farmer was just a pole made from a branch of a tree with a yoke at one end and a sharpened stick or piece of iron at the other which scratched the ground. A cross-piece made a simple handle for the plough-man.

As the ground was stony or perhaps on a hillside, two oxen dragged the plough by the yoke across their necks. The yoke had to be well made, otherwise it would hurt the animals. They were urged on by a long pole called a 'goad'. If the farmer was too poor to afford two oxen he sometimes yoked an ox and a donkey together.

The seed was scattered by hand from dawn to dusk and the ground was raked with a branch. Some seed fell on stony ground, and bad weather at sowing time meant a poor crop.

'For my yoke is good to bear'. Read the words of Jesus, Matthew 11: 28–30.

Read what happened when Elisha was ploughing (1 Kings 19: 19–21) and write the story in your own words.

'A sower went out to sow his seed'. Read Luke 8: 4–15.

Draw a picture of a man ploughing with oxen.

16

Harvesting

The barley harvest began in April and the wheat harvest in May or June, but the crops ripened earlier on the plains than in the uplands. When the crops were ripe, the men went into the fields and cut down the stalks, using iron reaping-sickles. A sickle is a curved knife.

The women helped by tying the stalks of corn into small bundles or sheaves and leaving them standing to dry in the sun. When the field was cleared, the poorest people were allowed to pick up any ears of corn that had fallen to the ground. This is called 'gleaning'.

An ancient law of the Hebrews said that the harvest should not be cut right up to the edges of the field, or the fallen ears of corn picked up, but that this should be left for the poor or for strangers.

So it was that, when the barley harvest began in Bethlehem, Ruth was allowed to glean in the fields of a rich man named Boaz.

Read the story of how a poor woman named Ruth gleaned in the fields of Boaz. Ruth 2: 1–9.

Rearrange the letters of these words to form the correct spellings: GGNINAEL; ENRGPAI; KCSLEI; THSAERV.

Read Mark 4: 26–32 and copy the parable of the mustard-seed.

'When you reap the harvest'. Read Leviticus 19: 9–10.

Threshing and winnowing

After the crop was gathered, the good grain had to be separated from the husks and stalks and this was done by 'threshing'. The sheaves of corn would be spread out on a hard, flat piece of ground called a threshing-floor. Here it was either beaten with sticks or crushed by a heavy sledge pulled by oxen. This was done in the open so that the wind would carry away the light husks.

Then, on a more windy day, the heaps of grain and chaff were tossed into the air with a large fork or shovel so that the chaff would be blown away and the heavier grain would fall to the threshing-floor. This is called 'winnowing'.

Finally, the grain was sifted and stored in a granary or barn. After winnowing, a farmer might sleep beside his grain to prevent its being stolen. In the time of David, it was the Philistines who robbed the threshing-floors of the Israelites (1 Samuel 23: 1).

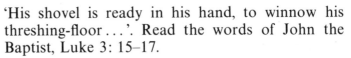

'His shovel is ready in his hand, to winnow his threshing-floor ...'. Read the words of John the Baptist, Luke 3: 15–17.

Write sentences about the work in the fields: ploughing; sowing; harvesting; threshing; winnowing.

David goes to the threshing-floor. Read 1 Chronicles 21: 18–26.

'Winnowed with shovel and fork'. Read Isaiah 30: 23–24.

Draw a picture-strip of men working in the fields.

Fishing

Jesus had many friends who were fishermen and fishing was an important trade. Some of the fish would be sold in the market, but large quantities were salted and packed into barrels for sale not only in other parts of Palestine, but for places as far away as Rome.

There were two kinds of fishing-nets. When Jesus found Andrew and Peter casting a net into the sea they were using a throwing-net (or cast-net). This was circular with weights all round the edge. As it was thrown over a shoal of fish the weights caused the net to open and fall flat on to the water, then, as the weights sank, the net closed to form a bag in which the trapped fish could be hauled in.

The other kind was a drag-net. This was very long with floats at the top edge and weights at the bottom so that, in the water, it was like a wall. Two boats, working together, would draw the two ends of the net together, gathering the fish inside it.

Jesus meets Andrew and Peter casting a throwing-net. Read Matthew 4: 18–20.

Read how two boats made a big haul of fish. Luke 5: 1–7.

Jesus talks about a fishing-net. Read Matthew 13: 47–48.

Describe the two kinds of fishing-nets.

Draw a picture of a man using a throwing-net.

Fishing on the lake

The Sea of Galilee is an inland lake 13 miles long and 8 miles wide at its widest point. Winds quickly whip down from the surrounding hills and stir the still waters into boiling waves.

Fishing boats on the lake were large enough to take four to six men, working as the crew. There was one sail only. This hung from a pole slung across the mast and could be quickly furled in sudden storms, the fishermen then taking to the oars.

Much of the fishing was done at night. The fishermen, in and out of the water, often worked naked. Once the fish were landed they were sorted carefully and the nets were dried and mended. James and John were working on their nets when Jesus called them to be disciples (Matthew 4: 21–22).

In the early days of the Church, when it was dangerous to be a Christian, the symbol of a fish was a secret sign among believers in Jesus.

The Storm on the Lake. Read Matthew 8: 23–27.

Read how Peter plunged into the sea to reach Jesus. John 21: 4–8.

Draw a picture of a Galilean fishing boat or, like the Christians of long ago, design a fish symbol as a secret sign.

Breakfast on the shore. Read John 21: 9–14.

Imagine you are a fisherman of Galilee and write a description of your boat and the work you do.

The carpenter

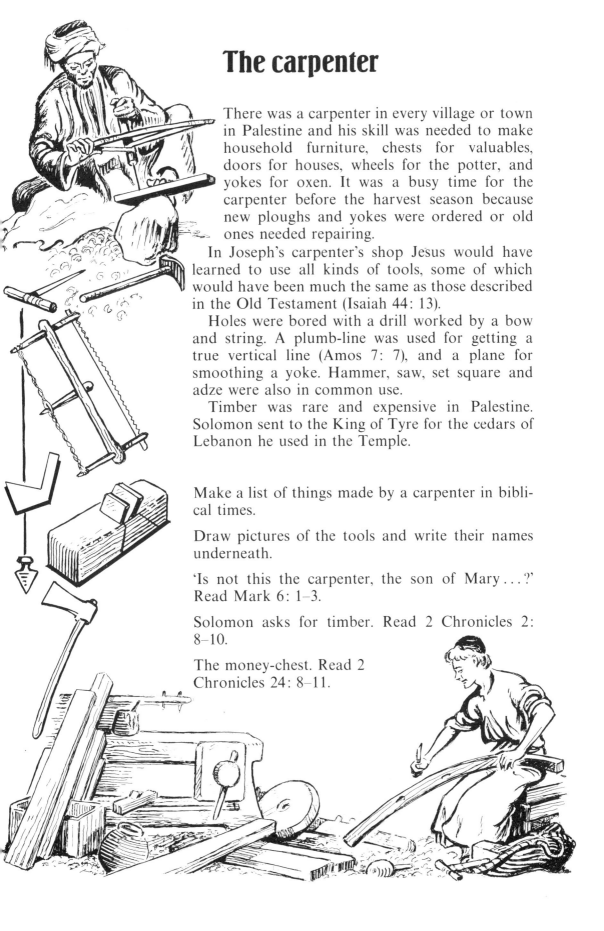

There was a carpenter in every village or town in Palestine and his skill was needed to make household furniture, chests for valuables, doors for houses, wheels for the potter, and yokes for oxen. It was a busy time for the carpenter before the harvest season because new ploughs and yokes were ordered or old ones needed repairing.

In Joseph's carpenter's shop Jesus would have learned to use all kinds of tools, some of which would have been much the same as those described in the Old Testament (Isaiah 44: 13).

Holes were bored with a drill worked by a bow and string. A plumb-line was used for getting a true vertical line (Amos 7: 7), and a plane for smoothing a yoke. Hammer, saw, set square and adze were also in common use.

Timber was rare and expensive in Palestine. Solomon sent to the King of Tyre for the cedars of Lebanon he used in the Temple.

Make a list of things made by a carpenter in biblical times.

Draw pictures of the tools and write their names underneath.

'Is not this the carpenter, the son of Mary . . . ?' Read Mark 6: 1–3.

Solomon asks for timber. Read 2 Chronicles 2: 8–10.

The money-chest. Read 2 Chronicles 24: 8–11.

The potter

Earthenware kept water pure and cool in a hot climate. Wine and olive oil were also kept in large clay vessels, so the work of the potter was very important.

The potter moulded his water pots from the clay he found in the valleys. First, he made the clay soft by treading and squeezing it. He then shaped the clay, with wet hands, by spinning it on a small wheel fixed by a rod to a larger wheel below, which he turned with his foot. The larger wheel made the small wheel spin faster. When he had got the shape he wanted, he stopped the wheel and released the pot by sliding a strand of hair under it.

When he had made a number of pots, he baked them in an oven, or kiln, to make them hard and ready for use. Sometimes, potters worked in groups making water jars, storage pots, plates, bowls and oil lamps.

Jeremiah goes to the potter's house. Read Jeremiah 18: 1–4.

Gideon's men smash 300 jars. Read Judges 7: 16–21.

Draw the shape of a jar and decorate it with a pattern.

The potter and his clay. Read Romans 9: 19–21.

'How to make a clay pot'. Write a description with this title.

22

The shepherd

Wherever you walked in these times you would see sheep and goats grazing together. They provided people with milk, meat, wool and skins, and therefore the work of the shepherd was very important.

The Eastern shepherd did not use dogs; he led his flock to fresh grasslands, calling each one by name. He carried a long staff curved at the end to guide them and a club to protect them against wild animals.

He took them to the well and drew water for them to drink. When other flocks arrived they would often get mixed up, so it was as well that the sheep answered to the voice of their own shepherd.

In the evening, the shepherd would gather his flock into the fold, an enclosure with rough stone walls and a single entrance. The shepherd would count each animal as it went in and then lie down to rest across the entrance to guard the open doorway. But before he could rest, the shepherd had to find any lost sheep.

'I am the good shepherd'. Read John 10: 11–16.

Read about the voice of the shepherd. John 10: 1–5.

The story of the Lost Sheep. Read Luke 15: 3–7.

Read Psalm 23, 'The Lord is my shepherd', and make a copy.

Make a small model of a sheep-fold with a single entrance.

The skill of the craftsman

In every Eastern city there were the shops of craftsmen, and streets were sometimes named after a particular craft or trade. The shops were just openings in the wall and much of the work was done in the open air.

The shoemaker's time was spent making and mending sandals. Slippers were made for indoor use. In the home, it was usual to wash a guest's feet on his arrival. Jesus washed the feet of his disciples in order to explain his teaching.

In the Street of Weavers, craftsmen worked the looms and made bright rugs and hangings. The blacksmith at his anvil made locks, cooking-pots, swords and axes. The copper-smith and silversmith worked with metal and the masons worked with stone. The King of Tyre sent stonemasons to Israel to build a house for David (2 Samuel 5: 11).

In Jerusalem there was a Street of Bakers who were confectioners as well. There was no trade or craft that could not be found in the narrow streets in biblical days.

Jesus washes the feet of his disciples. Read John 13: 3–11.

Each workman helps the others. Read Isaiah 40: 18–22 (New English Bible).

The skill of craftsmen. Exodus 35: 35.

Write the names, and the work they do, of all the craftsmen you can find.

Make a booklet with the title 'Daily Work in Biblical Times' and find out all you can from the previous pages.

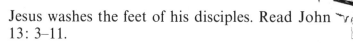

24

The market-place

Outside the city gate was the market-place where merchants set out their wares and sat on the ground before their stalls. Camels and donkeys, laden with farm produce, would be unloaded and travellers from distant parts would go to the money-changers to change their coins.

The scribe was there to write out letters and bills of exchange, for the market-place was also a court of law. Farmers and owners of vineyards came to hire labourers, and men sat by the gate begging for money.

Apart from the shepherd bringing in his sheep and goats to sell, there would be the sandalmaker and the copper-smith, the pedlar selling cheap trinkets and children playing around the stalls.

The Pharisees went there to look important and Jesus warned them of their pride.

All this would happen in the cool of the morning for, when the sun rose high, the crowds went home. But on the next day the busy market-place would come alive again.

A man came to the market-place to hire labourers for his vineyard. Read Matthew 20: 1–16.

Jesus warns the Pharisees. Read Luke 11: 37–43.

Write about all the things that happened in the market-place.

Read about the goods traded between countries of these times. Ezekiel 27: 12–24.

Draw a picture of a busy market-place.

25

ALL KINDS OF MEASURES

Money

In early times, all buying and selling was done by barter or exchange but, later, bits of metal were used for payment–the first coins.

The most common was a silver coin called a 'denarius'–known as a penny. The labourers who worked in the vineyards all day earned this coin. When Jesus asked to be shown the tax money it was a 'denarius' they gave him.

The Jews did not mint their own money but used coins that came from Tyre. The Temple tax could be paid only in this money, so there were money-changers in the Temple. Jesus upset their tables because they were making the Temple a 'robbers' cave'.

The smallest coin was the 'lepton'–worth about one-sixteenth of a penny. It was two of these coins the poor widow dropped into the box at the Temple.

The largest amount was the 'talent'. Silver and gold talents were worth so much that some men buried them under the ground for safe keeping.

The Pharisees try to trick Jesus. Read Mark 12: 13–17.

Read how Jesus drove the money-changers from the Temple. Mark 11: 15–17.

The widow who gave all she had. Read Mark 12: 41–44.

Draw a picture of the poor widow giving her coins.

Read Matthew 25: 14–30 and act a play to illustrate the story.

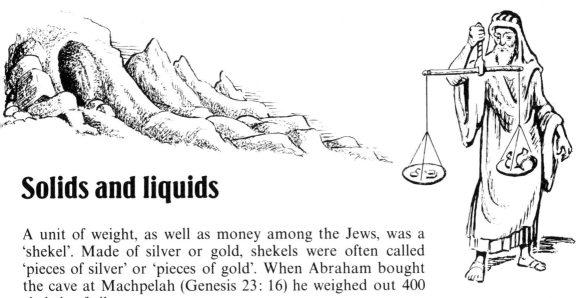

Solids and liquids

A unit of weight, as well as money among the Jews, was a 'shekel'. Made of silver or gold, shekels were often called 'pieces of silver' or 'pieces of gold'. When Abraham bought the cave at Machpelah (Genesis 23: 16) he weighed out 400 shekels of silver.

A shekel weight

The chief products of the Bible lands were corn, oil and wine. In dry measure an 'ephah' of corn would be about a bushel (a bushel in liquid measure equalled 5 gallons/23 litres). A 'log' of oil was equivalent to a pint (0.5 litres).

When Jesus went to the wedding feast at Cana-in-Galilee, the jars of wine there would each have held 9 gallons (41 litres). These measures were sometimes called 'firkins'. The water-pots at the wedding feast held 20 to 30 gallons (91–136 litres) each.

Eliezer gave two gold bracelets to Rebecca weighing 10 shekels. Read Genesis 24: 22–27.

Judas betrayed Jesus for thirty pieces of silver. Read Matthew 27: 1–5.

Read about the wedding feast at Cana-in-Galilee (John 2: 1–11), and write the story in your own words. Draw a picture to illustrate your story.

Length

If a man wanted to measure anything he used the 'cubit'. This was the length of his forearm from the elbow to the tip of the middle finger (about 20 inches/50 centimetres).

The width of four fingers made a 'palm', and three palms were a 'span' (about 10 inches/25 centimetres).

An 'acre' in the Bible (Isaiah 5: 10) really means the amount of land that could be ploughed in one day by a yoke of oxen.

A mile, in New Testament times, was the Roman mile or a thousand double paces. A Roman law said that any Roman soldier could make any person carry his pack for him – but no farther than one mile.

Greater distances were measured by the distance a man could travel in so many days. Laban put three days' journey between himself and Jacob when he took the flock (Genesis 30: 36). The distance between Jerusalem and the Mount of Olives was a sabbath day's journey, but it was against the Jewish law to travel farther than 2000 cubits on the sabbath.

Going the second mile. Read Matthew 5: 39–42.

King Solomon built a Temple for the Lord 60 cubits long. Read 1 Kings 6: 2–3.

The apostles went a sabbath day's journey to Jerusalem. Read Acts 1: 12–14 and write a list of their names.

Write the names of money, weights and measures already mentioned, along with their modern counterparts.

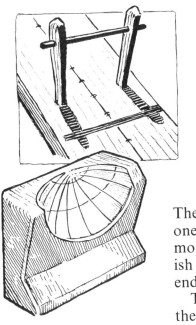

Telling the time

The Jews reckoned the length of each day from one sunset until the next–'The evening and the morning were the first day' (Genesis 1:5). The Jewish sabbath begins on the Friday at sunset and ends on Saturday at sunset.

The hours were measured by the shadow cast by the sun on a sundial or shadow clock.

The daylight hours in biblical times were divided into twelve, so that noon, when the sun was at its highest, was called the sixth hour. This would differ according to the seasons.

The night was divided into three parts (or watches) by the Jews, but into four by the Romans. These were evening, midnight, 'cock-crowing' and early morning. During the night that Jesus was arrested, Peter disowned him three times before the hour of 'cock-crowing' (Luke 22:61).

Answer these questions:
When does the Jewish sabbath begin and end?
Name the four Roman nightwatches.
Where would a sundial be placed?

Peter denies knowing Jesus. Read Luke 22:54–61.

The shadow moves on the sundial. Read 2 Kings 20:8–11.

'One day speaks to another'. Read Psalm 19:1–6 and copy in your best handwriting.

ANIMALS OF BIBLE LANDS

The camel

A camel was a useful animal in biblical times because it is stronger than a horse and can work for long hours in the desert. Its padded feet do not sink deeply into the sand, its hump is a storehouse of food for long journeys and it can go for days without water. It can eat prickly plants and bitter weeds and its eyes and nostrils can keep out the sand. It has been rightly called 'the ship of the desert'.

A camel can carry a load of 5 hundredweight (250 kilograms, as well as the rider) and travel, on average, 28 miles a day. It was bred for speed as well as work; the desert tribes made 'hit-and-run' raids on the Israelites, escaping on swift camels.

Owning many camels was a sign of great wealth, and Job, the 'greatest man in all the East', had 3000 of them (Job 1: 2–3).

The hair was used for clothing, and John the Baptist had a coat of camel's-hair (Mark 1: 6).

Jesus spoke of a camel in one of his parables. Read Matthew 19: 23–26.

Joseph was sold by his brothers to a camel-caravan of merchants. Read Genesis 37: 25–28.

Read about the camel raids of desert tribes, Judges 7: 12.

Write all you know about a camel.

Trace the outline of a camel and repeat it several times to make a picture of a camel-caravan.

The donkey

Donkeys have been used to carry men and heavy burdens from the earliest times, and there are pictures of them on wall-paintings dated about 1895 B.C. The animals are called 'asses' in the Bible, and without this beast of burden Abraham could not have made his long journey from Babylonia, nor could Joseph and Mary have travelled to Bethlehem and then escaped to Egypt.

Carrying heavy loads, the patient donkey could pick its way carefully in hilly country and live on less food than the horse. Sometimes it helped the farmer by pulling the plough, later carrying the produce to market. Kings and important people rode through the streets on white donkeys when on peaceful journeys, and Jesus chose a donkey to carry him into Jerusalem amid the shouts of those who welcomed him as King.

Read the story of Balaam and his donkey. Numbers 22: 22–35.

Jesus enters Jerusalem on a donkey. Read Matthew 21: 1–11.

Make a list of some of the ways a donkey might have been used in the stories of the Bible.

'The ass and the lion'. Read 1 Kings 13: 23–29.

Copy the picture of the wall-painting of an ass.

Beasts of the field

Oxen appear early in the Bible and they were used for work and for food in the time of Abraham: for pulling the plough, treading corn, turning the grinding wheels at the mill and for pulling carts. They often worked in pairs as a 'yoke of oxen'.

Sheep, also, were valuable to the Hebrews and their wool has been used from the time of Moses. They provided meat and milk, and the lamb was always the most important animal for sacrifice at the Temple. A ram's horn was sometimes used as a trumpet (Joshua 6: 1–5).

Goats and sheep were herded together in biblical times. Jacob spent many years looking after his uncle's flock. Goats could feed in places where sheep could not reach. Like sheep, goats were used for meat and milk. Their milk could be made into cheese. Goat's hair was woven into cloth and the skin made garments and water-bottles.

'Six covered wagons and twelve oxen'. Read Numbers 7: 1–5.

Abraham offers a ram as a sacrifice to God. Read Genesis 22: 1–13.

'As a shepherd separates the sheep from the goats'. Read the words of Jesus, Matthew 25: 31–40.

Write four sentences about the work of oxen.

Answer these questions:
    Why were sheep valuable to the Hebrews?
    Who spent many years looking after goats and sheep?
    In what ways were goats useful?

Wild beasts

Shepherds always had to be on the alert for wild animals, like the wolf, which could scatter a flock and kill many of the sheep. David must have seen wolves when he looked after his father's sheep, and Jesus warned his disciples that he was sending them out 'like sheep among wolves' (Matthew 10: 16).

The fox was also common and lived in caves or holes and raided the vineyard. Thorn hedges were put round vineyards because foxes like fruit and they ate the grapes when they were ripe. Jesus spoke of foxes having their holes and the birds their roosts and, because Herod was cunning, Jesus called him 'that fox'.

In the Bible, jackals are sometimes called foxes and, as they hunt in packs, it was the jackals that Samson used when he set light to the cornfields of the Philistines.

Read about the bad shepherd who ran away from the wolf (John 10: 12–13) and draw a picture of this happening.

'Foxes have their holes...'. Read the words of Jesus (Matthew 8: 18–20).

Samson put 300 jackals into the cornfields. Read Judges 15: 3–5.

Draw a picture of a fox raiding a vineyard.

Shaggy beasts

When lions lived in Bible lands they preyed on other wild animals like deer, wild boar and antelope. In winter, when food was hard to find, lions might attack the flocks of sheep, as David found when he was a shepherd. A man named Benaiah 'went down into a pit and killed a lion on a snowy day' (1 Chronicles 11: 22).

Lions are not found today in Palestine, but they are mentioned in many books of the Old Testament. A man from Judah was killed by a lion on the road from Bethel (1 Kings 13: 24), and Daniel was thrown into a lions' pit because he worshipped God.

The phrase 'When a man runs from a lion and a bear meets him' (Amos 5: 19) means that a bear could be more dangerous than a lion. When cornered, a bear can be very dangerous. The bear of the Old Testament is the Syrian bear and it is lighter coloured than the Brown bear of other lands.

'Daniel is saved from the den of lions'.
Read Daniel 6: 19–23.

Draw a picture of a man fleeing from a lion and meeting a bear.

'The Lord who saved me from the lion and the bear'. Read 1 Samuel 17: 37–40.

'The young lions roar for prey'. Read Psalm 104: 19–25 and copy verses 20–22.

Small creatures

There are not many poisonous snakes in Bible lands, but the viper can be dangerous. St Paul was bitten by a viper on the island of Malta when he was collecting sticks for a bonfire. He came to no harm and the people thought he was a god.

There are many frogs and lizards. One of the plagues of Egypt was of frogs, which overran the land and invaded houses.

Locusts are a kind of grasshopper. They swarm together in many millions, flying like a huge black cloud. When they come down to feed they eat everything green and ruin the crops. A plague of locusts came to Egypt at the time of the Exodus.

Locusts can be cooked and eaten, and John the Baptist ate locusts when he was in the wilderness (Mark 1: 6).

When St Paul was bitten by a viper. Read Acts 28: 1–6.

Read about the plague of frogs in Egypt. Exodus 8: 1–13.

Write three sentences about the locust.

Read about the damage that locusts can do. Exodus 10: 13–15.

Draw pictures of a snake and frogs.

The birds of the air

Birds fly in their thousands as they migrate over the lands of the Bible in spring and autumn. Jeremiah tells of the stork, the crane, and the swallow that 'know the time of their coming', and the Israelites fed on small birds called quail as they crossed the desert. These birds, flying low over the desert, are easily tired and they came down in great numbers.

Noah set free a raven and a dove from the Ark to find out whether the floods were going down and the cooing of the turtle-dove was heard when winter had gone (Song of Songs 2: 11–12).

In the swampy marshes lived the pelican, with its large pouch, and the heron, which spears fish with its sharp, pointed beak. The vulture and the hawk were birds of prey in the biblical period as they are today, and the desert owl lived among ruins in the wilderness (Psalm 102: 6).

'You are worth more than any number of sparrows'. Read Matthew 10: 29–31.

Rearrange the letters of the names of these birds to form the correct spelling: LWSOWLA; AQLIU; NAPCEIL; NRVEA; NHOER.

Make a list of as many birds as you can find in the Bible.

'The stork in the sky'. Read Jeremiah 8: 7–8.

Read about the hawk and the vulture. Job 39: 26–30.

36

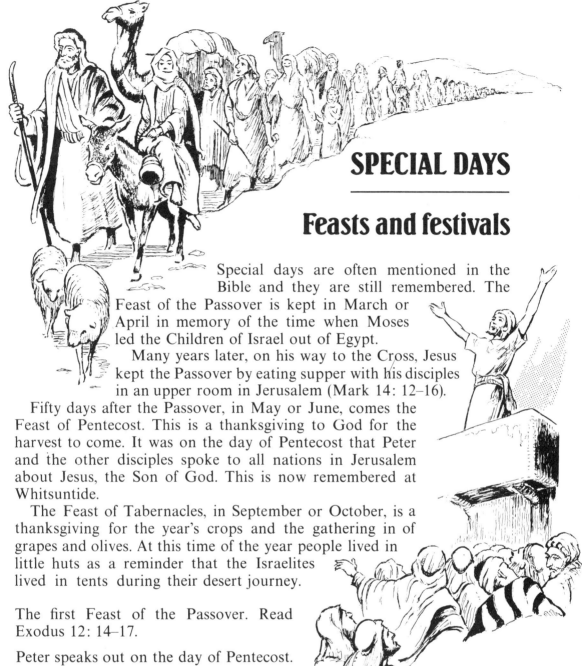

SPECIAL DAYS

Feasts and festivals

Special days are often mentioned in the Bible and they are still remembered. The Feast of the Passover is kept in March or April in memory of the time when Moses led the Children of Israel out of Egypt.

Many years later, on his way to the Cross, Jesus kept the Passover by eating supper with his disciples in an upper room in Jerusalem (Mark 14: 12–16).

Fifty days after the Passover, in May or June, comes the Feast of Pentecost. This is a thanksgiving to God for the harvest to come. It was on the day of Pentecost that Peter and the other disciples spoke to all nations in Jerusalem about Jesus, the Son of God. This is now remembered at Whitsuntide.

The Feast of Tabernacles, in September or October, is a thanksgiving for the year's crops and the gathering in of grapes and olives. At this time of the year people lived in little huts as a reminder that the Israelites lived in tents during their desert journey.

The first Feast of the Passover. Read Exodus 12: 14–17.

Peter speaks out on the day of Pentecost. Read Acts 2: 1–4 and 22–24.

Write sentences to explain the meaning of Passover and Pentecost.

The Feast of Tabernacles. Read John 7: 1–9.

Draw a picture of a hut used at the Feast of Tabernacles.

A day of gladness

The Jewish people loved festivals, especially a wedding which was a happy time of music and dancing. Friends and neighbours were invited and everyone wore their best clothes. Not to do so was an insult to the families concerned.

The bride's dress was the finest of all, and she wore her best jewels and bracelets on her wrists and ankles. Tiny bells hung from her head-dress and strings of coins from her forehead.

The wedding procession took place at night and everyone carried lighted torches or lamps. There was much laughing and singing, with the blowing of trumpets, clashing of cymbals and beating of drums.

The merry-making would go on for days and the guests were given wine to drink. This was why Mary asked Jesus to help when the wine ran out at the wedding feast at Cana-in-Galilee (John 2: 1–11).

The parable of the Wedding Feast. Read Matthew 22: 1–14.

Ten girls went out to meet the bridegroom. Read Matthew 25: 1–13.

Write about a wedding in biblical times.

'Be ready for action'. Read Luke 12: 35–40.

Draw a picture of the bride.

The Sabbath

The Hebrew word 'shabath' means 'to cease' and the sabbath (Saturday) is kept by the Jews as a holy day–the day to cease work.

The Jewish sabbath, the seventh day, lasts from sunset on Friday to sunset on Saturday. By the end of the first century A.D., Christians had made the first day of the week (Sunday) their holy day because Jesus rose from the dead on a Sunday.

In the time of Jesus, the Pharisees kept very strict laws about the sabbath. Some laws were foolish, such as forbidding a knot to be tied on that day. The Pharisees quarrelled with Jesus because he did not keep the sabbath as strictly as they wanted. Jesus taught them that 'the sabbath was made for the sake of man and not man for the sabbath'.

'Keep the sabbath day holy'. Read the commandment, Deuteronomy 5: 12–15.

Read how Jesus cured a man on the sabbath (John 5: 1–18).

The Pharisees accuse the disciples of breaking the sabbath by plucking ears of corn. Mark 2: 23–27.

Draw a picture of the disciples in a cornfield.

Complete these questions:
The Jewish sabbath is on a . . . . . .
Christians made . . . . . . their holy day.
Sunday is the . . . . . . day of the week.

With instruments of music

In biblical days musical instruments were used in worship and rejoicing. Their chief function was to accompany singing and dancing, people clapping their hands to the time of the music (Psalm 47: 1).

Cymbals were clashed together and the 'sistrum', or rattle, was shaken. The 'timbrel', or 'tabret', was a simple tambourine used with cymbals. All these were percussion instruments.

The harp was a stringed instrument with six to nine strings, while the 'psaltery' had three wooden sides and ten strings. It was David who played the harp to King Saul when the king was unhappy.

A simple trumpet was made from the horn of a ram, and there were straight metal trumpets and 'cornets' used to call people together. These were wind instruments.

The most common instrument was the pipe or flute played by the lonely shepherd. This was made of reed with finger-holes like those in a recorder.

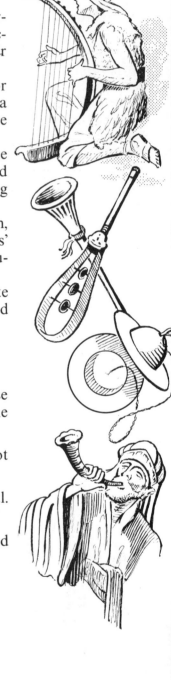

Harp, trumpet and cymbals. Find these instruments in Psalm 150. Copy the psalm in your own handwriting.

'We piped for you and you would not dance'. Read Luke 7: 32.

David played the harp for King Saul. Read 1 Samuel 16: 14–23.

Draw pictures of a harp, trumpet and cymbals.

THE FRUITS OF THE EARTH

Grapes

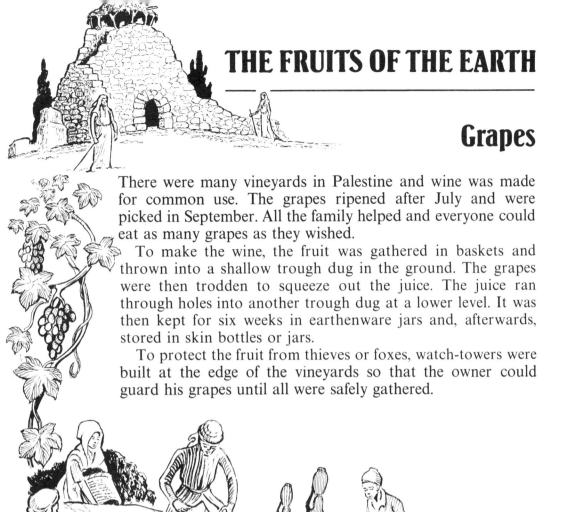

There were many vineyards in Palestine and wine was made for common use. The grapes ripened after July and were picked in September. All the family helped and everyone could eat as many grapes as they wished.

To make the wine, the fruit was gathered in baskets and thrown into a shallow trough dug in the ground. The grapes were then trodden to squeeze out the juice. The juice ran through holes into another trough dug at a lower level. It was then kept for six weeks in earthenware jars and, afterwards, stored in skin bottles or jars.

To protect the fruit from thieves or foxes, watch-towers were built at the edge of the vineyards so that the owner could guard his grapes until all were safely gathered.

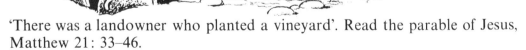

'There was a landowner who planted a vineyard'. Read the parable of Jesus, Matthew 21: 33–46.

Read the story of the labourers who worked all day in the vineyard. Matthew 20: 1–16.

'I am the true vine ....'. Read the words of Jesus (John 15: 1–6).

Describe, in your own words, how wine was made in these times.

Draw a picture of a watch-tower.

Olives

The most important tree in biblical times was the olive-tree, and olives have been called the 'meat and butter' of Palestine.

We first hear about the olive in the story of Noah. It tells of the dove flying out from the Ark over the water to seek dry land and returning with an olive-leaf in her beak (Genesis 8: 10–11).

The olive is a beautiful tree, blossoming white in springtime with silvery-grey leaves which do not fall in winter. A good tree can yield as much as 10 to 15 gallons (45–68 litres) of olive oil–enough for a family until the next harvest.

From olive-wood Solomon had two great doors and carvings made for the Temple (1 Kings 6: 31–32) and, at that time, gave the King of Tyre 1800 gallons of olive oil every year.

Jesus crossed the Mount of Olives (or Olivet) on his way to Jerusalem (Matthew 21: 1–5).

The olive-tree in God's house. Read Psalm 52: 8–9.

'When one beats an olive-tree'. Read Isaiah 17: 6 (New English Bible).

The trees wanted a king. Read Judges 9: 8–15 and write the story in your own words.

Draw a picture of the dove returning to the Ark with an olive-leaf in her beak.

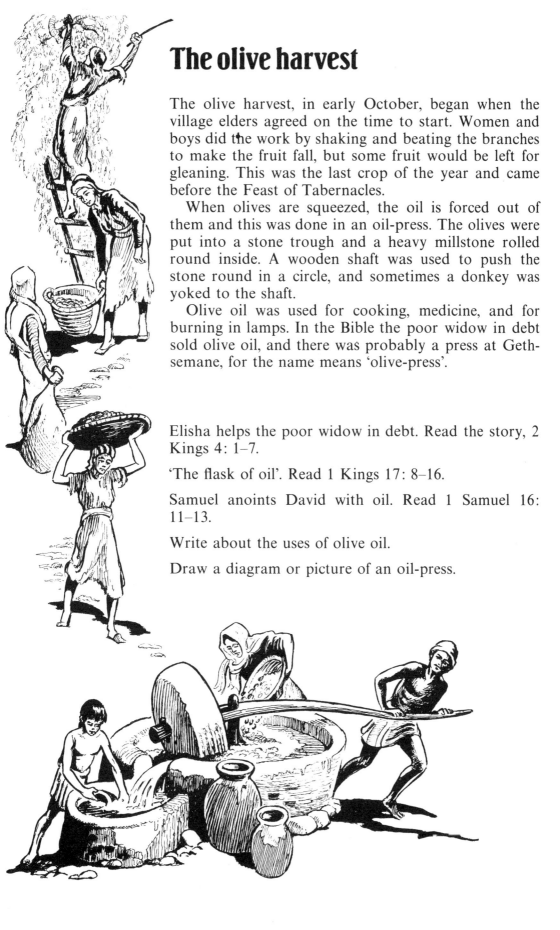

The olive harvest

The olive harvest, in early October, began when the village elders agreed on the time to start. Women and boys did the work by shaking and beating the branches to make the fruit fall, but some fruit would be left for gleaning. This was the last crop of the year and came before the Feast of Tabernacles.

When olives are squeezed, the oil is forced out of them and this was done in an oil-press. The olives were put into a stone trough and a heavy millstone rolled round inside. A wooden shaft was used to push the stone round in a circle, and sometimes a donkey was yoked to the shaft.

Olive oil was used for cooking, medicine, and for burning in lamps. In the Bible the poor widow in debt sold olive oil, and there was probably a press at Gethsemane, for the name means 'olive-press'.

Elisha helps the poor widow in debt. Read the story, 2 Kings 4: 1–7.

'The flask of oil'. Read 1 Kings 17: 8–16.

Samuel anoints David with oil. Read 1 Samuel 16: 11–13.

Write about the uses of olive oil.

Draw a diagram or picture of an oil-press.

Trees of the Bible

There were more trees in Palestine, long ago, than there are today. Cedars were of great value and Solomon used them to build his Temple and palaces. They came from Lebanon and the logs were taken to the coast and floated in rafts to the seaport of Joppa.

The oak-tree, or 'terebinth', was also well known. Joshua put up a great stone under an oak-tree to remind the Israelites of their promise to God, and Absalom, the son of David, was caught in the branches of an oak-tree when riding a mule (2 Samuel 18: 9).

The fruit of the fig-tree was very valuable as a food. The main harvest was in September. Jesus told a parable about the fig-tree (Mark 13: 28–31), and when choosing his disciples, it was under a fig-tree that he saw Nathanael.

King Solomon brings cedars from Lebanon. Read 1 Kings 5: 1–9.

The promise to God made under an oak-tree. Read Joshua 24: 26–28 and draw a picture of an oak-tree and stone.

Read how Jesus saw Nathanael under a fig-tree, John 1: 43–51, and write down all the names mentioned.

Find out and write the names of the twelve disciples. Read Luke 6: 13–16 and check your list of names.

GOING ON A JOURNEY

Transport

The roads over the hills in Bible lands were winding tracks strewn with stones and boulders. It was dangerous to travel alone and people travelled together for safety. Jews from every part made the journey to Jerusalem at the times of the great festivals. Merchants, too, travelled together to sell their goods in the cities, and their lines of camels following each other were called 'caravans'.

Poor people went on foot or rode on donkeys. Others were carried on a litter or drove a two-wheeled cart pulled by a mule. Sometimes, the Romans used a four-wheeled carriage or, for speed, rode in a chariot. The slow-moving wagon was used by country folk for carrying heavy loads.

When the Romans built roads, travel became easier. These roads were paved and sometimes marked with milestones.

Mary, Joseph and Jesus went to Jerusalem for the Passover. Read Luke 2: 41–52.

'Carry no purse or pack, and travel barefoot'. Read the words of Jesus to his disciples (Luke 10: 1–9).

Draw a picture of a chariot or wagon.

'So Naaman came with his horses and chariots'. Read 2 Kings 5: 9–14.

Write three paragraphs to describe a caravan, a litter and a wagon.

Inns

If a traveller came to a shepherd's tent or to a village his host brought him water to wash his feet and gave him food and a bed for the night. There were very few inns along the roads. Some were little more than four walls round a well where travellers could spend the night, sheltering from the weather and robbers. A fire would be lit in the courtyard and there the men and their beasts would sleep. They would bring their own food with them and set off early the next morning on their journey.

Other inns were more comfortable. An innkeeper lived over the gate and provided meals for travellers who could pay for them (Luke 10: 35). There were stables for animals and in Bethlehem the stables were probably built into the rock. In the manger of one of these the infant Jesus was laid, because there was no room at the inn.

The story of the Good Samaritan. Read Luke 10: 30–37 and write the story in your own words.

'No room in the inn'. Read Luke 2: 1–16.

Draw and colour a picture, or make a model, of the first Christmastide at Bethlehem.

A visitor is made welcome. Read Genesis 24: 29–32.

Write a story, or act a play, about the inn at Bethlehem.

Famous Bible journeys

To escape from Herod, Joseph took Mary and the baby Jesus on the long road from Bethlehem to Egypt, and not until Herod was dead did they return to Nazareth (Matthew 2: 13–15).

The Jews did not like travelling through Samaria because the Samaritans hated them, and when he was a man Jesus found no shelter in a Samaritan village because he was going to Jerusalem (Luke 9: 51–56).

Once, on the road to Jericho, Jesus healed a blind man and later, in the city, stayed at the house of Zacchaeus.

When his friends thought he had left them, Jesus came up and walked with two of them on the road to Emmaus. It was on a desert road that Philip met a man in his carriage and baptized him at a roadside pool (Acts 8: 26–38), and Paul heard the voice of Jesus on the road to Damascus (Acts 9: 3).

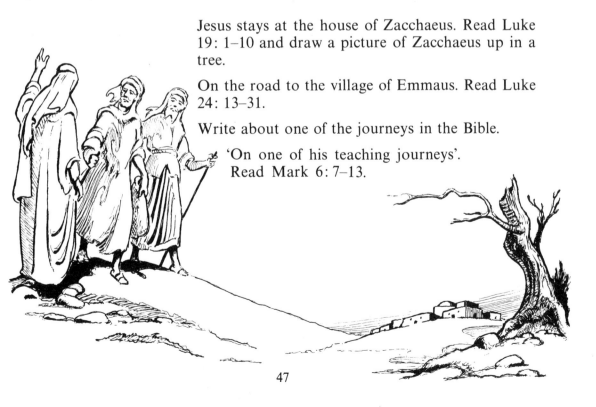

Jesus stays at the house of Zacchaeus. Read Luke 19: 1–10 and draw a picture of Zacchaeus up in a tree.

On the road to the village of Emmaus. Read Luke 24: 13–31.

Write about one of the journeys in the Bible.

'On one of his teaching journeys'. Read Mark 6: 7–13.

Sea voyages

The Israelites rarely went to sea, but their neighbours the Phoenicians were fine sailors and sailed to many lands.

The ships that sailed from Bible lands were high in the bows and in the stern, and were driven by one big sail and oars. Sometimes they used smaller sails as well. The ships were steered by two paddle-rudders and, as the compass had not yet been invented, the sailors were guided by the stars.

There were also lighthouses, and one at Alexandria was built of marble with a beacon always burning at the top.

Many ships took corn from Egypt to Rome, and the largest could be 180 feet (55 metres) in length and take 276 passengers. St Paul must have travelled nearly 10 000 miles by land and sea to spread the good news of Jesus. He made three great sea voyages and once was shipwrecked on the island of Malta.

'They that go down to the sea in ships'. Read Psalm 107: 23–32.

The shipwreck on the island of Malta. Read Acts 27: 39–44.

Draw a picture of a ship in biblical times.

Complete these sentences:
    Ships took ...... from Egypt to Rome.
    The ships were steered by ......
    There was a lighthouse at ......
    St Paul made .... sea voyages.

The voyage of Jonah. Read Jonah 1: 1–17.

THE ROMAN ARMY

Soldiers

At the time of Jesus there were many soldiers of the Roman army in the streets of the towns and cities. The Romans had become rulers of Palestine not long before Jesus was born. The Jews hated them and longed for a leader who would drive them out.

It was by order of a Roman emperor that Joseph and Mary went to Bethlehem 'to be counted' and, later, Jesus was arrested by Roman soldiers at Gethsemane.

A Roman soldier wore a helmet and armour. His shield was made of wood and leather and he carried a short sword and spear. An officer in command of a hundred soldiers was called a 'centurion'. Jesus healed the servant of a centurion at Capernaum.

The Jews hated the standards carried by the Roman regiments, for they reminded them of heathen gods. Because of this, the Romans did not usually take them into Jerusalem.

Jesus heals the centurion's servant. Read Luke 7: 1–10.

The Roman soldiers arrest Jesus at Gethsemane. Read John 18: 1–11.

Draw a picture of a Roman soldier.

The centurion at the Cross. Read Luke 23: 44–48.

Write a description of a Roman soldier.

Siege weapons

When the Roman legions swept through Palestine and took Jerusalem they made Herod 'King of the Jews'.

In a 'legion' in the Roman army there were 6000 men. This was divided into ten 'cohorts'. A cohort was divided into six centuries (six companies, each of a hundred soldiers).

The Romans used many weapons to attack cities. The three main types were the catapult, ballista and battering-ram.

The catapult had a heavy wooden frame carrying a beam with a weight at one end. The beam was pulled down by a rope and then released. It struck a huge dart or arrow on top of the frame.

The ballista threw iron bolts or stones. It could throw a large stone 400 yards (366 metres).

The battering-ram broke down walls or doors. It was a heavy pole slung on a carriage with wheels. The roof of the carriage protected the attacking soldiers.

Jesus is taken before Herod. Read Luke 23: 6–12.

Complete these sentences:
    A legion had ...... men.
    Each legion had ...... cohorts.
    A centurion was in command
    of ...... soldiers.

Draw a picture of a Roman siege weapon.

'Cornelius, a centurion in the Italian Cohort'. Read Acts 10: 1–8.
'Get ready two hundred infantry'. Read Acts 23: 23–35.

PLACES THAT JESUS KNEW

Nazareth and Bethlehem

Nazareth was a town on the hills of Galilee, overlooking the trade routes from the Jordan valley to the coast of the Great Sea (the Mediterranean). Jesus lived in Nazareth as a boy and it was here that he 'grew big and strong and full of wisdom' (Luke 2: 40).

When he was older, he returned to Nazareth and spoke in the synagogue there, but the angry local people tried to throw him over the brow of the hill on which the town was built.

Today, women still draw water from Mary's Well at Nazareth.

The name Bethlehem means 'House of Bread'. It is a town 5 miles south of Jerusalem and it was the early home of David (1 Samuel 17: 15). Ruth and Naomi returned here to a kindly welcome.

Jesus was born in Bethlehem and the hills nearby have always been used by shepherds for grazing their sheep.

Jesus at Nazareth. Read Luke 4: 16–30 and Mark 6: 1–6.

Draw a picture of the Well at Nazareth.

Samuel anoints David at Bethlehem. Read 1 Samuel 16: 1–13.

Ruth and Naomi return to Bethlehem. Read Ruth 1: 16–19.

Write short descriptions of Nazareth and Bethlehem and draw a map to show their positions.

A Synagogue

A 'synagogue' was a place in village or town where people could go to worship God. The word means 'gathering together'.

A synagogue is a simple building and when people met there on the sabbath the Laws were read. The scrolls of the Law were kept in a large chest or cupboard called the Ark. There was a veil in front of the Ark and above it a lamp which was always kept burning. There was also a many-branched candlestick.

The service was led by the 'ruler of the synagogue' and consisted of psalms, prayers and readings. Anyone could be called to explain the Scriptures, and Jesus often spoke in the synagogue services (Matthew 4: 23).

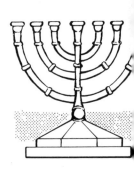

A school for children was also held in the synagogue of each village, and when Paul travelled to spread the Gospel he spoke first to the Jews he met in the synagogues (Acts 17: 1–4).

Jesus cures a man in the synagogue. Read Mark 1: 21–28.

The man with the withered arm. Read Luke 6: 6–11.

Make up your own service with hymns, prayers and readings.

'When you pray'. Read Matthew 6: 5–15.

From cardboard boxes, make a model of a synagogue.

Jerusalem

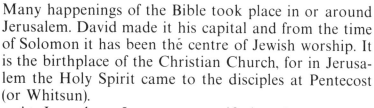

Many happenings of the Bible took place in or around Jerusalem. David made it his capital and from the time of Solomon it has been the centre of Jewish worship. It is the birthplace of the Christian Church, for in Jerusalem the Holy Spirit came to the disciples at Pentecost (or Whitsun).

At Jerusalem, Jesus was crucified and rose again. Near the Temple stood the castle of the Roman Governor from which Peter escaped and where Paul was saved from the mob.

In that city, Jesus told a blind man to wash in the Pool of Siloam and he was cured, and at the Sheep Pool a crippled man walked again.

The 'Old City' of Jerusalem lies between two valleys, with the Mount of Olives to the east. It is built on hilly ground, has narrow streets, and the walls have been rebuilt many times.

Peter escapes from the castle. Read Acts 12: 1–10.

The crippled man at the Sheep Pool. Read John 5: 1–9.

Find out more things that happened in Jerusalem.

Copy the plan of the city.

When Jesus was a boy in Jerusalem. Read Luke 2: 41–52.

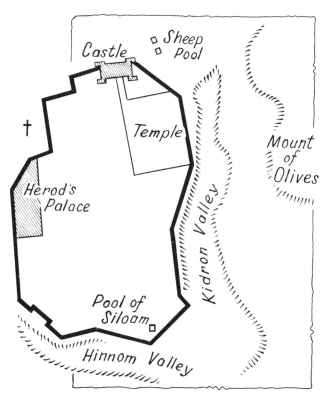

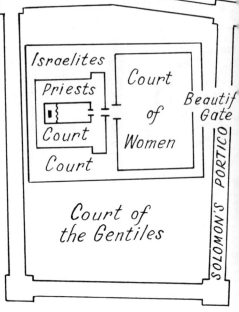

The Temple at Jerusalem

When David took Jerusalem his son Solomon built the first Temple in the city. It was destroyed in 586 B.C., and a second Temple was built in the same place. Herod the Great built the third Temple in Jerusalem, and this was the Temple that Jesus knew.

The east side of the Temple was called Solomon's Portico, and it was here that Jesus walked and the Jews threatened to stone him. Here, too, was the Beautiful Gate where Peter healed the crippled man.

This gate led to the Court of Women and then to the Israelites Court where only men could go. The Priests' Court surrounded the Holy Place which led, through a curtain, to The Holy of Holies. The curtain was once torn in two from top to bottom (Matthew 27: 50–51).

The Temple was a beautiful building of white marble. Some parts were splashed with gold.

Jesus is threatened in the Temple. Read John 10: 22–31.

Peter heals the cripple at the Beautiful Gate. Read Acts 3: 1–11 and write about what happened.

Draw a plan of the Temple.

Jesus cleanses the Temple. Read John 2: 13–22.

THINGS WHICH ARE WRITTEN

Bible writings

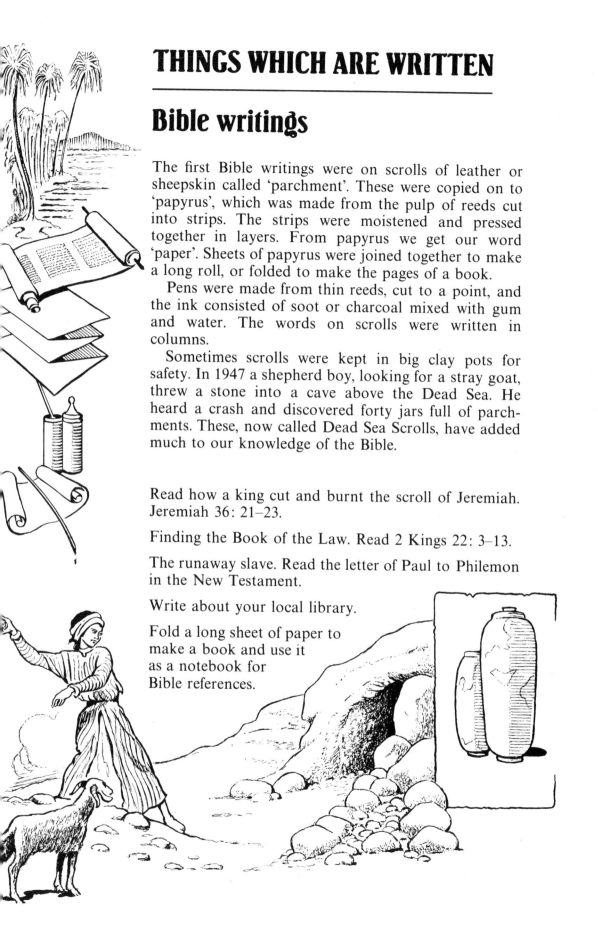

The first Bible writings were on scrolls of leather or sheepskin called 'parchment'. These were copied on to 'papyrus', which was made from the pulp of reeds cut into strips. The strips were moistened and pressed together in layers. From papyrus we get our word 'paper'. Sheets of papyrus were joined together to make a long roll, or folded to make the pages of a book.

Pens were made from thin reeds, cut to a point, and the ink consisted of soot or charcoal mixed with gum and water. The words on scrolls were written in columns.

Sometimes scrolls were kept in big clay pots for safety. In 1947 a shepherd boy, looking for a stray goat, threw a stone into a cave above the Dead Sea. He heard a crash and discovered forty jars full of parchments. These, now called Dead Sea Scrolls, have added much to our knowledge of the Bible.

Read how a king cut and burnt the scroll of Jeremiah. Jeremiah 36: 21–23.

Finding the Book of the Law. Read 2 Kings 22: 3–13.

The runaway slave. Read the letter of Paul to Philemon in the New Testament.

Write about your local library.

Fold a long sheet of paper to make a book and use it as a notebook for Bible references.

How we got our Bible

The Bible is a library of sixty-six books ('biblia' is a Greek word for 'books'). There are thirty-nine books in the Old Testament and twenty-seven books in the New Testament.

The books of the Old Testament are over 2000 years old and were written before the time of Jesus. Most of the books were written in Hebrew on to scrolls rolled on handles to make reading easier.

The books of the New Testament were written in Greek by Christians of the first century A.D. Originally the writings were on separate scrolls. They were not made into books until the fourth century A.D.

The Bible was translated into Latin by Jerome in the fifth century. It is called the 'Vulgate' from a Latin word meaning 'made common'.

The Bible can now be read in over a thousand languages.

Complete these sentences:
>   There are ...... books in the Bible.
>   The Old Testament was written before the time of ....
>   The New Testament was written in the ...... language.
>   'Vulgate' means ....

Answer these questions:
>   What is the first book of the Old Testament?
>   Name the four Gospels.
>   Why were the scrolls rolled on handles?
>   When did Jerome translate the Bible into Latin?

'Take a scroll and write on it every word ...'. Read Jeremiah 36: 1–5.

How many names of the books in the Bible can you remember? Make a list.

IXθYC

Signs and symbols

Secret signs were used by the first Christians because, long ago, it was dangerous to be known as a follower of Jesus.

The fish was used as a symbol because the Greek word for fish (ichthus) spells out the Greek initials of the words Jesus, Christ, God's Son, Saviour.

Another sign was the 'chi-rho'. This was a joining of the first two letters of the Greek word for Christ.

The anchor sign was used by the Early Christians in underground caves called 'catacombs'. It may have been used because it looks like a cross or because of the words in the Bible–'That hope we hold. It is like an anchor for our lives ...' (Hebrews 6: 19).

The letters 'INRI' are the initials of the Latin words for 'Jesus of Nazareth King of the Jews'. They were the words written by Pilate and fastened to the Cross on which Jesus was crucified.

Read about the words written by Pilate. John 19: 19.

Copy the secret signs used by the Early Christians.

As a follower of Jesus, imagine that you lived long ago and make up you own secret sign.

Write, in your own words, about the secret signs of the first Christians.

Map of Palestine

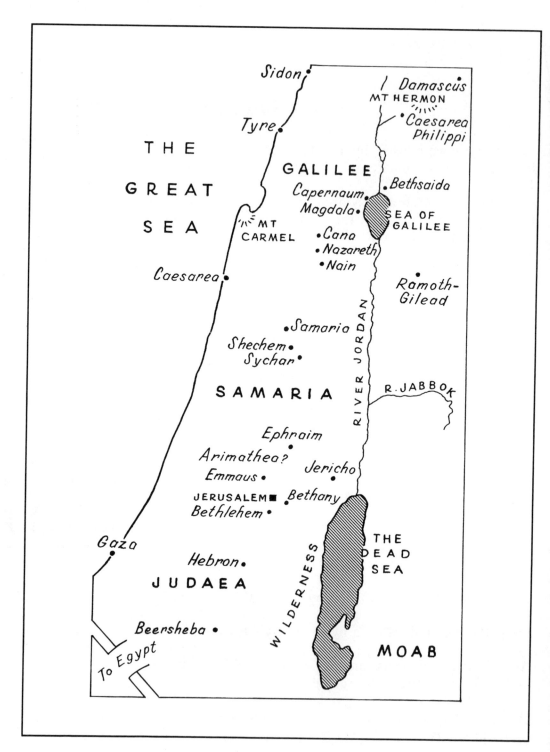

People and places

ARIMATHEA A place to the north-west of Jerusalem and the home of Joseph, a secret disciple of Jesus.

BEERSHEBA A frontier town of Israel, where Abraham dug a well.

BETHANY Village on the east slope of the Mount of Olives, where Mary and Martha lived.

BETHLEHEM Early home of David. Jesus was born here.

BETHSAIDA A fishing town at Galilee. The home of Peter, Andrew, James, John and Philip.

CAESAREA Central depot for Roman troops.

CAESAREA PHILIPPI Where Peter first realized that Jesus was the Messiah.

CANA Village in Galilee near Nazareth. The scene of the first miracle of Jesus.

CAPERNAUM Where Jesus taught in the synagogue and healed many people.

CARMEL, MOUNT Here Elijah challenged the prophets of Baal.

DAMASCUS One of the oldest cities in the world. Paul saw a vision of Jesus on the road to this city.

DEAD SEA A sea that is so salty no fish can live in it.

EMMAUS Two disciples were walking towards this village on the first Easter Sunday, when Jesus joined them.

EPHRAIM Jesus stayed here shortly before his entry into Jerusalem.

GALILEE, SEA OF A freshwater lake, part of the River Jordan water-way.

GAZA The story of Samson took place here.

HEBRON An ancient city, and David's first capital.

HERMAN, MOUNT A snow-capped mountain. Its melting snows are the main water-supply for the River Jordan.

JERICHO First captured by Joshua. Jesus stayed here at the home of Zacchaeus.

JERUSALEM The city of David, centre of Jewish worship in the Temple and birthplace of the Christian Church.

JORDAN, RIVER The great river of Palestine flowing for 100 miles from Mount Hermon to the Dead Sea.

MAGDALA On the caravan route from Nazareth to Damascus.

NAIN A small village where Jesus restored to life the son of a widow.

NAZARETH A town on the hills of Galilee where Jesus spent his boyhood.

RAMOTH-GILEAD Where King Ahab of Israel was killed in a battle with the Syrians.

SAMARIA Jews tried to avoid this city when travelling from Galilee to Judaea.

SHECHEM Where Joshua called the tribes of Israel together to remind them of God's goodness.

SIDON Jesus visited its borders and Paul saw friends here while on his way to Rome as a prisoner.

SYCHAR Jesus helped a Samaritan woman at Jacob's Well near the town of Sychar.

TYRE Jesus visited the neighbourhood and Paul once landed at this port.

Can you remember?

1   What is a 'tallith'?
2   Which colour was the most expensive to use in biblical times?
3   Where did this colour come from?
4   How many jewels were on the breastplate of a High Priest?
5   What did each jewel represent?
6   What did the King of Babylon give to Daniel?
7   How did the four friends help the paralysed man?
8   In biblical times, how were rooms warmed in winter?
9   How did they grind corn into flour?
10   How did they make butter?
11   In what months did the rain fall in Canaan?
12   What was a 'shadoof'?
13   How did a water-seller carry the water?
14   Where did Jesus tell the blind man to go and wash?
15   What are 'nomads'?
16   When they were pulling a plough, how were oxen urged on?
17   When did the wheat harvest begin in Bible lands?
18   Who gleaned in the fields of a man called Boaz?
19   Name two kinds of nets used by fishermen on the Sea of Galilee?
20   What was the length and width of the Sea of Galilee?
21   What was used to get a true vertical line?
22   Where did the potter bake his pots to make them hard?
23   Where were sheep kept at night?
24   Where would you often find a market-place?
25   What was the most common silver coin called?
26   For how much money did Judas betray Jesus?
27   What was the length of a 'cubit'?
28   How were the hours measured in biblical times?
29   Because it is useful in the desert, what has the camel been called?
30   What was a pair of oxen called?
31   What was put round a vineyard to stop foxes from entering?
32   Who killed a lion in a pit on a snowy day?
33   Who was bitten by a viper on the island of Malta?
34   What birds did Noah set free from the Ark?
35   Why is the Feast of the Passover kept?
36   When in biblical times did a wedding procession take place?
37   At what times does the Jewish sabbath begin and end?
38   What was a 'psaltery'?
39   When was the grape harvest?
40   What have olives been called?

41 What does the name 'Gethsemane' mean?
42 What trees did Solomon use to build his Temple?
43 On what road did the Good Samaritan help the injured man?
44 Where was there a lighthouse in biblical times?
45 What was a Roman officer called who was in command of a hundred men?
46 How many Roman soldiers were there in a legion?
47 Where did Jesus live as a boy?
48 What biblical city is the birthplace of the Christian Church?
49 Where did Peter heal the crippled man?
50 From where do we get the word 'paper'?
51 How many books are there in the New Testament?
52 What do the initials 'INRI' stand for?

Answers

1   A 'tallith' is a prayer shawl.
2   Purple was the most expensive colour.
3   The colour came from a shellfish caught in the sea.
4   There were twelve jewels on the breastplate of a High Priest.
5   One of the twelve tribes of Israel.
6   The King gave Daniel a purple robe and a chain of gold.
7   They broke through the roof to get the sick man to Jesus.
8   Rooms were warmed by burning charcoal or wood in braziers.
9   In a corn-mill between two large stones.
10 By shaking goat's milk in a large leather bag.
11 The rain fell twice a year – in October and March.
12 A weighted pole, with a bucket at one end to raise water.
13 In a goatskin bag, carried on his shoulder.
14 In the Pool of Siloam.
15 Nomads are wandering people, moving with their flocks and herds.
16 By a long pole called a 'goad'.
17 The wheat harvest began in May or June.
18 Ruth gleaned in the fields of Boaz.
19 A throwing-net (cast-net) and drag-net.
20 The Sea of Galilee was 13 miles long and 8 miles wide.
21 A plumb-line was used to get a true vertical line.
22 The potter baked his pots in an oven or kiln.
23 At night, the sheep were kept in a fold.
24 A market-place was often outside the city gate.
25 The most common silver coin was called a 'denarius'.
26 Judas betrayed Jesus for thirty pieces of silver.
27 The length of the forearm from elbow to tip of the middle finger.
28 The hours were measured by the shadow cast by the sun.
29 The camel has been called 'the ship of the desert'.
30 A yoke of oxen.
31 Thorn hedges were put round vineyards.
32 Benaiah went down into a pit and killed a lion on a snowy day.
33 St Paul was bitten by a viper on the island of Malta.
34 Noah set free a raven and a dove from the Ark.
35 To remember the time when Moses led the Israelites out of Egypt.
36 A wedding procession took place at night.
37 From sunset on Friday to sunset on Saturday.
38 A psaltery was a type of harp with ten strings.
39 The grape harvest was in September.
40 Olives have been called the meat and butter of Palestine.

41   The name Gethsemane means 'olive-press'.
42   Solomon used the cedars of Lebanon to build his Temple.
43   On the road from Jerusalem down to Jericho.
44   There was a lighthouse at Alexandria.
45   A centurion was in command of a hundred men.
46   There were 6000 Roman soldiers in a legion.
47   As a boy, Jesus lived in Nazareth.
48   Jerusalem is the birthplace of the Christian Church.
49   Peter healed the crippled man at the Beautiful Gate.
50   We get the word paper from a reed called 'papyrus'.
51   There are twenty-seven books in the New Testament.
52   Jesus of Nazareth King of the Jews.